HOME MOSAICS

HOME MOSAICS

Contents

Introducing mosaics

Mosaic design has often been described as "painting by numbers," and however basic a description this might be, it does provide a clue to this art form's key attraction—its accessibility. Mosaics are simply the creation of patterns and pictures from pieces of stone, ceramic, porcelain, or glass … what could be simpler?

Mosaic designs range from very simple to very detailed—both can be beautiful. Start with straightforward designs, and as you gain confidence, move on to more ambitious projects. Experiment with different materials and patterns.

You will soon discover why mosaics have existed as an art form for over 2000 years—some of the earliest examples of mosaics are from ancient Mesopotamia, and are believed to date back to around 3000 b.c. Their combination of decorative and functional attributes have ensured that this versatile and durable art form has a timeless appeal. All you need to enjoy mosaic design is time, patience, and imagination.

MATERIALS

Tesserae (which comes from the Latin word for "square" and the Greek word for "four") is the name of the pieces used to make mosaics. They come in all shapes and sizes, and are supplied loose or on sheets. When storing tesserae, you need to make them easily identifiable, so glass or transparent containers are ideal for loose cubes, and clearly labeled boxes work well for flat sheets. All adhesives, cements, and additives are best stored in a dry, cool place.

Here is a list of the main materials used in mosaic design. However, there are no rules, and mosaicists can use any number of other materials, including glass beads, buttons, coins, shells, slate, semiprecious stones, and broken household china.

MARBLE Available in a natural palette of colors, marble tesserae have either polished or unpolished finishes: the former gives a smooth, elegant look, whereas the latter has a more rustic appeal. Cut marble using a hammer and hardy (see page 8) and protect with a sealant. Commonly used pieces are ⅝ x ⅝in (1.5 x 1.5cm).

VITREOUS GLASS Available in many colors, these are relatively cheap and resistant to heat and frost, making them ideal for both interior and exterior use. Cut glass using mosaic nippers (see page 8). They are usually supplied in single-color sheets of ¾ x ¾in (2 x 2cm), or loose in bags of mixed colors.

PORCELAIN These are usually supplied unglazed and are available in numerous colors. Suited to both internal and external application, they have excellent slip-resistant properties even when wet. Use mosaic nippers to cut them (see page 8) and seek advice from your tile supplier regarding sealants.

CERAMIC These are similar to porcelain tesserae except that they are usually glazed.

SMALTI These are made from glass, which is prepared and cut into rectangular strips and then into rectangular tesserae. The irregularities of the hand-cut glass surfaces reflect light beautifully. Sold in 1lb (500g) or 2lb (1kg) bags, usually in ½ x ⅝in (1 x 1.5cm) pieces, smalti are relatively expensive but worth every cent. They can be used internally and externally because they are resistant to heat and frost. Use a hammer and hardy to cut them (see page 8).

GOLD OR SILVER LEAF To make these tesserae, a thin layer of 24-carat gold or silver is hammered onto a colored glass backing and covered with a veneer of glass. This is then hand cut into tesserae, which can lead to irregularities in size and shape. They are available with either a flat or rippled surface. Use them for decorative purposes only, because the silver or gold breaks down in conditions such as extreme heat and frost.

PEBBLES AND STONES These are available in a variety of colors, sizes, and textures. Granite and other hard stones are recommended for their durability, and they can be used internally and externally.

HOUSEHOLD CERAMIC TILES These come in many colors and sizes. They are inexpensive, which makes experimental cutting affordable. Always check the durability of the tiles, because certain types are prone to cracking under extreme conditions.

GLASS AND MIRROR Use these to add a reflective quality to your mosaics. They are available in large panels from glass and some tile suppliers, and should be cut very carefully with glass cutters.

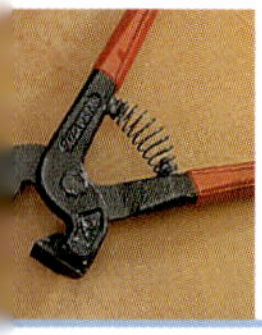

Basic tools and techniques

The basic mosaic tool kit is very simple, and you may already have some of this equipment around your home. If not, visit a hardware store, builder's supplier, or tile supplier.

1. HARDY This is used with a hammer for cutting marble and smalti. The hardy is a small metal block with a chisel-type blade, which can either be embedded in concrete in a flowerpot or in an upright log.

2. HAMMER This is curved on one edge and tipped with tungsten carbide for durability. There are various weights of hammer—choose one that feels comfortable to you and is in proportion with the hardy.

3. MOUTH AND NOSE FILTER MASK Wear this when cutting tesserae, mixing grout and cement, or using strong-smelling solvents.

4. MOSAIC NIPPERS These are used to cut vitreous glass, porcelain, and ceramic tesserae. The cutting edge is usually tipped with tungsten carbide for durability. Buy nippers with spring-action handles to make cutting less arduous.

5. TILE CUTTERS These cutters carve through tiles in a two-step process. One part of the cutters has a small wheel or blade; the other part has a flat edge known as the snapper. First, the tile is scored with the blade; then, it is "snapped" with the flat edge.

6. ELECTRIC DRILL This is used for attaching mosaic projects to walls or other surfaces. Buy a selection of plastic wall anchors and screws, and invest in a countersink bit, which hides screw-heads. A jigsaw is also a useful tool for delicate, intricate cutting.

7. GUMMED BROWN PAPER When dampened, the gum bonds tesserae temporarily, which is ideal for the indirect method (see page 11). You can also use plain brown paper, but you will need to apply gum glue to the matte side.

8. WOOD Used as a base material or support, the type of wood you use will depend on the weight and size of your mosaic project, and whether it will be used inside or outside. Always prime before use.

9. PAINTBRUSH/GLUE SPREADER These are used to paint/prime surfaces and apply glue.

10. POLYVINYL ACETATE (PVA) GLUE This is excellent for priming or preparing surfaces.

11. TAPE MEASURE/RULER Measuring tools.

12. LEVEL This has a liquid measure with a bubble in it. When the bubble is central in the liquid, the surface being measured is straight.

13. SAFETY GLASSES Wear these when cutting tesserae, as slivers can damage your eyes.

14. SCISSORS Cutting tool for paper/card.

15. GUM GLUE This is a water-based adhesive. It is applied to plain brown paper when using the indirect method (see page 11).

16. TWEEZERS These are wonderful for picking up small tesserae and positioning them, or for removing unwanted pieces.

17. AWL This makes an excellent "pricking-out" implement for removing unwanted cement and mosaics.

18. CRAFT KNIFE Cutting tool for paper/card.

19. STRING Useful for creating large circles.
20. Masking tape This is not as sticky as adhesive tape, so it is ideal for attaching templates to tracing paper temporarily.

21. GRAPH AND SKETCH PAPER These are especially useful during the design stages.

22. MARKERS, PENS, AND PENCILS Use markers to draw your design on the base material. Pens and pencils are essential throughout.

SAFETY ADVICE

When cutting

- wear surgical gloves, safety glasses, and a mouth and nose filter mask
- wear close-toed shoes
- lay drop cloths if working inside

When applying adhesives, grouts, and sealants

- follow manufacturers' instructions
- wear surgical or rubber gloves
- work in well-ventilated areas; use a filter mask if necessary
- wear an apron or smock
- lay drop cloths

When drilling

- always unplug when changing bits
- wear safety glasses

Cutting and scoring

MOSAIC NIPPERS:

These are used to cut vitreous glass and porcelain tesserae. Hold the nippers in one hand and the tessera in the other. Before cutting, get used to handling the nippers, which should be held toward the bottom of the handles. Place the tessera face up between the cutting edges of the nippers and then apply firm pressure.

CUTTING IN HALF Place the tessera halfway into the mosaic nippers. Squeeze the handles firmly and the tessera will break in half. If you need quarters, repeat the procedure with half a tessera. The quarters can also be cut in half to create smaller tesserae that are ideal for outlining.

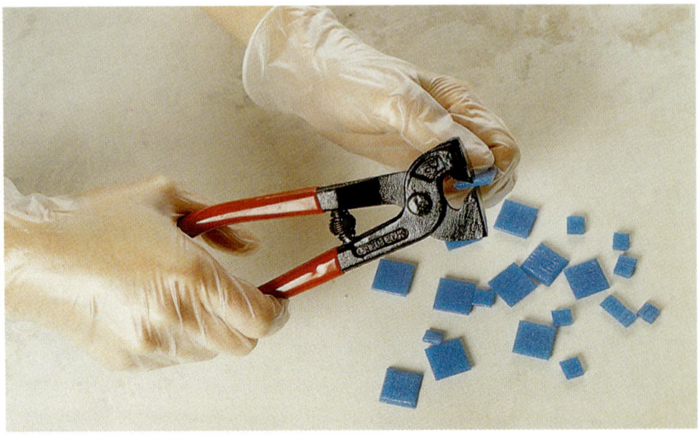

CUTTING DIAGONALS Place the tessera diagonally between the cutting edges of the nippers. Apply pressure and the piece should break into two triangles.

CUTTING CURVES OR CIRCLES This shape is slightly more difficult to perfect than halves or diagonals, but can be achieved if you nip off each corner of the tessera. Then, slowly "nibble" all the way around the tile to produce a smooth circular or oval shape.

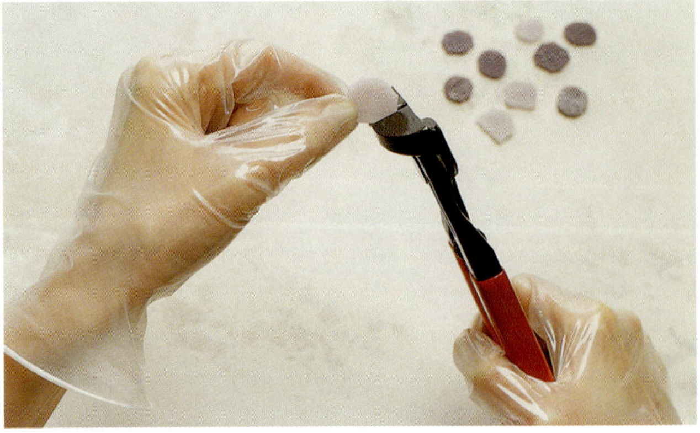

HAMMER AND HARDY: Used to cut smalti and marble, this is similar to a tool used by the Romans. Make sure that your cutting hand is not restricted while you work and be patient—perfect results take time.

Position the tessera over the blade of the hardy where you want the cut to be. Bring the hammer down lightly and firmly on the center of the tessera. Avoid inhaling dust by not cutting directly under your nose.

TILE CUTTERS:

These are useful if you want to cut ceramic tiles that measure more than 1in (2.5cm) square, and are ideal if you are using spare tiles left over from the bathroom or kitchen. The cutters have a dual function: first, the blade scores a line along the tile; then, the snappers break it. For ceramic squares, cut strips and then score and snap them into squares. You can get larger cutters or cutting machines for cutting thicker, tougher tiles.

SCORING TILES To produce a scored line on a ceramic tile, place a metal ruler in the exact position that you want the cutting line to be. Then run the tile cutters' blade along the edge of the metal ruler, applying even pressure as you go.

SNAPPING TILES Put the tile cutters' "snappers" over the center of the scored line. Use your other hand to take the pressure away from the cut. Apply firm pressure to the cutters until you hear a snapping noise when the tile is cut.

Adhesives, grouts and tools

There are different types of adhesives and grouts available and it is important that you choose the correct one for your project's requirements.

1. POLYVINYL ACETATE (PVA) GLUE A white glue available in two forms: water soluble and non-water soluble. The former can be used in the direct method. Also used to prime surfaces.

2. GUM GLUE This is usually water soluble and is used for the indirect method (see page 16).

3. CEMENT-BASED ADHESIVE This is available in powder, ready-mixed, or rapid-setting forms. Using an additive will allow more movement and flexibility.

4. MORTAR (not illustrated) Made from sand, cement, and water, this is ideal for exterior floor mosaics. The ratio is generally 3:1 coarse sand to cement.

5. GROUT Used to fill the gaps between the tesserae, this comes in ready-mixed or powder form and in a variety of colors. The cement-based powder form is illustrated here. Ready-made products are also available, but they tend to leave a residue behind.

6. EPOXY GROUT (not illustrated) This is a two-part, resin-based grout that creates a waterproof barrier.

7. PAINT SCRAPER This can be used to mix and apply small amounts of adhesive and grout.

8. NOTCHED TROWEL Used for laying adhesive, the notched edge combs the adhesive to ensure an even layer and create a good tooth for the tiles to bond to. A ¼in (3mm) trowel is recommended because it creates a smaller grooved bed that is ideal for mosaics.

9. TROWEL Use a pointed trowel for applying adhesive in small, awkward areas, and for measuring and mixing adhesive and grout.

10. MARGIN TROWEL Square-headed trowel.

MIXING CEMENT AND GROUT

Measuring ingredients Follow the manufacturers' instructions with regard to quantities and ratios of ingredients—you can use various measuring devices, such as one full trowel or one full measuring cup to represent one unit of material.

Adding water Pour the ingredients into a clean bucket. Slowly add water and additive, and mix with a trowel.

Smoothing the mixture Using a small trowel, mix the ingredients thoroughly. The texture should be smooth and free from lumps, and neither too runny, nor too thick.

11. PALETTE KNIVES Available in different-shaped heads, this flexible tool is great for applying adhesive or grout in small areas, and for smoothing and removing excess.

12. PROTECTIVE GLOVES Use rubber gloves when cleaning and grouting, and surgical gloves when applying adhesive and cutting tesserae.

13. GROUT FLOAT OR SQUEEGEE Used for applying grout, especially on large projects, and for removing grout residue.

14. CLOTH Use for polishing grout residue.

15. TILER'S SPONGE Fine-grained sponge ideal for removing grout and cleaning. Use circular movements to ensure even coverage.

16. SEALANT A wide variety of sealants are available—seek advice from a tile supplier for the product most suited to your project.

17. ADDITIVE FOR ADHESIVE This is added to powder adhesive to allow greater movement. It is especially important when working on wood and floorboards.

18. ADDITIVE FOR GROUT This is used with powder grout to increase the grout's flexibility. Read the label for safety advice.

19. MEASURING CUPS Used when measuring ratios of water, grout, and adhesive.

Direct mosaic-laying method

As the name suggests, this method involves applying the tesserae "directly" (face up) into position. This technique is useful because it enables you to see the final work progress piece by piece. It is used mostly in three-dimensional projects, on uneven surfaces, in mosaic murals, and backsplashes. It is not recommended for flat surfaces because the results may be irregular.

1 Run some sandpaper wrapped around a block of wood across the surface you are going to tile to provide a good tooth for the adhesive to bind to. Sand any rough edges.

2 Paint the front and side edges with one coat of PVA glue to prime the surface. Make sure you clean your brush immediately after use or it will become stiff.

3 While you are waiting for the glue to dry, start to cut the mosaic pieces (see page 8) and prepare the adhesive. Once the glue has dried completely, draw your design on the primed surface with a pencil or marker pen.

4 Spread the adhesive onto the base using a palette knife (or a notched trowel for large projects). Put the tesserae in place following the outline of the design. Allow the cement-based adhesive to dry for 24 hours.

5 Prick out excess cement with an awl or similar tool. If you leave it, it will be visible through the grout. Wash it away with a sponge and water. If using marble tesserae, apply a coat of marble protector.

6 Put on rubber gloves and mix a quantity of grout (see page 9). Use a palette knife, squeegee, or paint scraper to squeeze the grout in the gaps between the tiles. Use a grout float for large projects.

7 Using a clean, damp sponge, remove the excess grout. Repeat this process several times, and rinse the sponge regularly to keep it clean and avoid smearing.

8 Use a cloth to polish the surface and remove any residue. Allow the grout to dry for 24 hours, then apply a sealant with a paintbrush or cloth. This is particularly important if the mosaic is made of marble.

Indirect mosaic-laying method

The indirect method involves laying the mosaics in reverse: draw the design back to front on gummed brown paper and stick the tesserae in position. When the mosaic is complete on paper, apply it to the permanent base in a bed of adhesive. Wash off the paper to reveal the design, then grout. Use this method for flat surfaces and large projects.

1 Draw your design. Trace onto tracing paper, turn the paper over, then transfer the design onto brown paper (sticky or matte side up) with the design in reverse.

2 Stick the tesserae in position face down on the paper. For gummed paper, use water to bond the tesserae. For plain paper, use a water-soluble glue, such as gum glue.

3 Prepare some cement-based adhesive using the method outlined on page 9. Apply to the surface using a paint scraper, or a trowel for large projects. Prime the surface before you begin, especially if using wood.

4 Drag a notched trowel at a 45° angle toward you in one sweeping action. This creates a grooved surface in the adhesive, which provides a good tooth into which the tesserae can bond.

5 Carefully lift the mosaic and align its top edge with the top of the wood. Slowly lower the mosaic onto the adhesive. Smooth and press the tesserae with your hands. Allow to dry for 24 hours.

6 To reveal the design, moisten the paper with a wet sponge and then peel it off. Remove excess cement by "pricking" it out with an awl or similar tool. If using marble, apply a marble protector at this stage.

7 Wearing rubber gloves, prepare and apply grout, then remove any excess with a damp sponge. Rinse the sponge frequently or you will simply smear the grout instead of removing it. Allow to dry for 24 hours.

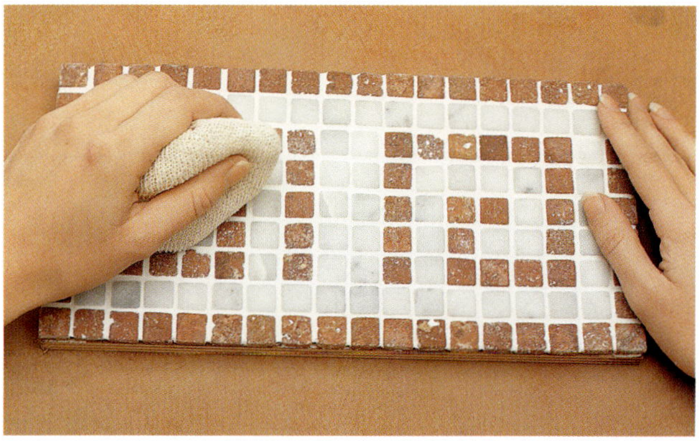

8 Polish the mosaic with a cloth to remove the fine layer of grout residue, then apply a sealant with a paintbrush or cloth. This is particularly important if the mosaic is made of marble.

LIVING ROOMS & DINING ROOMS

Japanese sushi table

TOOLS AND MATERIALS

Pencil
Ruler
Level
Sandpaper and block
Surgical and rubber gloves
Table: 35in (90cm) long x 22in (55cm) wide
Vitreous glass tesserae: ¾ x ¾in (2 x 2cm)
Mosaic nippers
Safety glasses and mask
PVA glue and paintbrush
Gummed brown paper, or plain brown paper and gum glue: 24in (60cm) long x 16in (40cm) wide or the size of your table
Two buckets and a trowel
Awl or similar tool
Notched trowel: ⅛in (3mm)
Sponge and cloth
Gray powder adhesive and additive
White powder grout and additive
Clear marine varnish
Black latex paint
Tracing paper

GLASS TESSERAE COLORS

Brown
Fire engine red
Pebble gray
Misty white
Shiny black
Charcoal

This beautiful, Japanese-inspired sushi table will look very stylish in any home. To create it, either use an existing table and reinvent it, or make a new one from scratch. The geometric pattern on the tabletop reflects a simple, abstract Zen style that creates an interesting focal point at meals and provides a perfect backdrop to the delights of the Japanese delicacy of sushi—dainty packages of seaweed, rice, and raw or cooked fish. The pattern consists mainly of vertical and horizontal rectangles and lines. The colors have been limited to black, white, gray, and one of the primary colors, red. This would be a good choice of project for a beginner, because it uses whole squares and gently introduces you to cutting the squares in half. If you are updating an existing table, make sure that you paint the legs with black paint and varnish to give a sleek, lacquer finish.

Using the template

Trace the template at the back of the book using tracing paper. Turn the tracing paper over and draw over the outline of the design on the reverse in pencil. Turn it back over and place it on top of some brown paper. Trace over the lines once again, transferring the design onto the brown paper. If you are using an existing table, as in the example pictured here, you may find that the template does not cover the full tabletop. If so, use the direct method on page 10 to add a border around the template design, which should be positioned in the center.

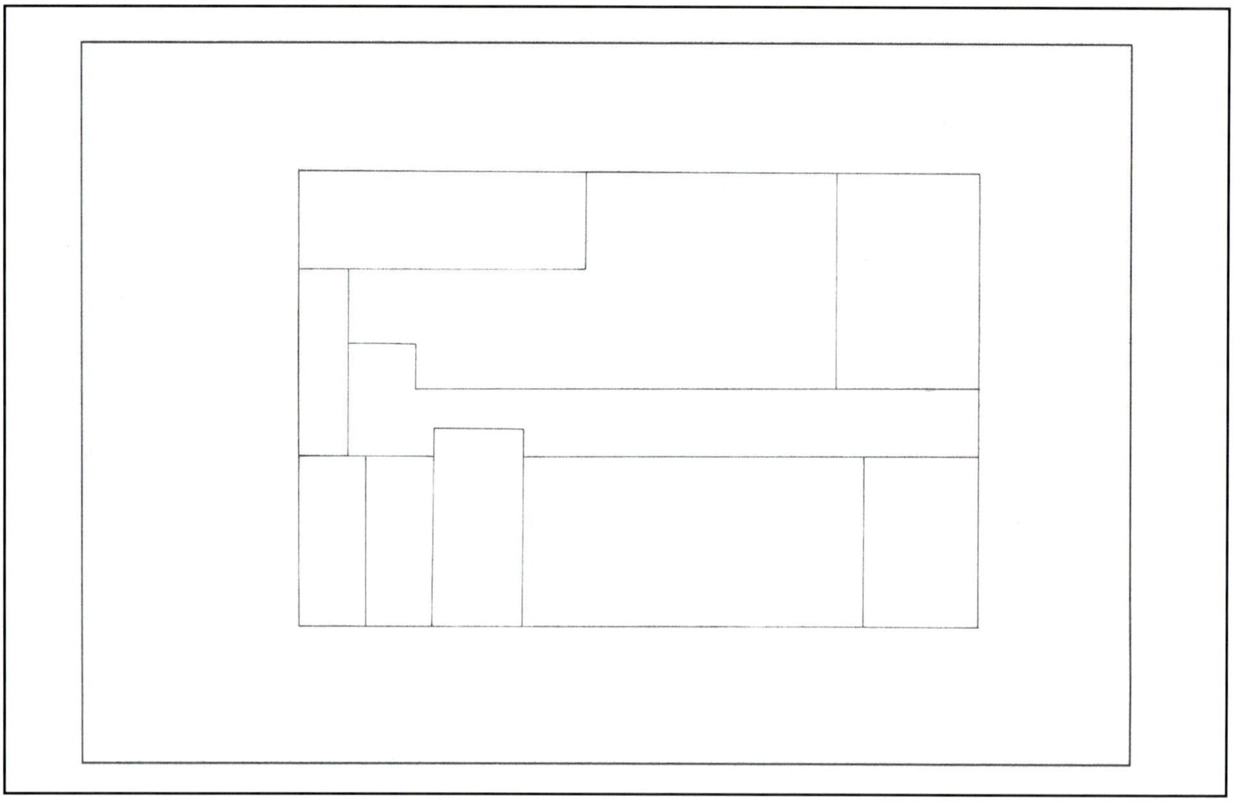

1 Using sandpaper and a block, sand the surface of the tabletop. Then prime it with PVA glue, using a paintbrush. If you are updating an old table, ask at your hardware store which adhesive and primer will work best with the materials.

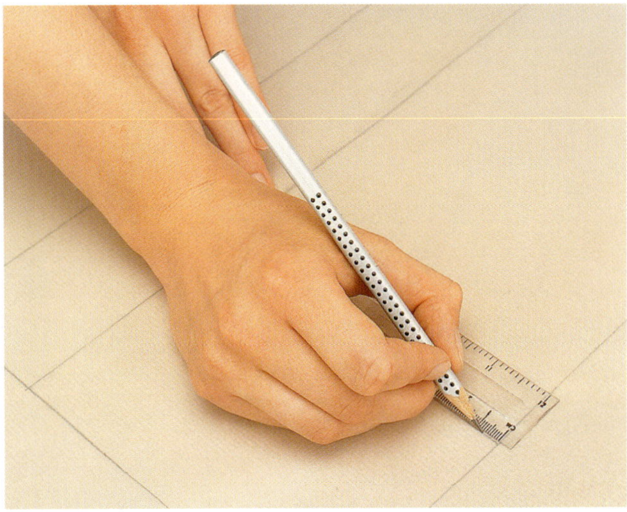

2 Trace the template design onto brown paper. Turn the paper over and mark a center point, using a ruler and pencil, to ensure that the template is in the center when you stick it down onto the table.

3 Cut the pebble gray, shiny black, and charcoal tesserae in half using mosaic nippers (see page 8 for an explanation of the cutting technique and page 7 for safety advice). Leave the red and white mosaics whole. Then, using a damp sponge on gummed brown paper or gum glue on plain brown paper, stick the tesserae into position face down. Complete the pattern and allow to dry.

4 If your existing tabletop is larger than the template, mark a cross in the center of the table. This should match the center point drawn on the brown paper in step 2. Draw in the full template rectangle: 24in (60cm) long x 16in (40cm) wide.

5 Mix some adhesive and spread it inside the drawn rectangle using a trowel. Groove the adhesive with a notched edge of the trowel and place the mosaics that you stuck to the brown paper into the adhesive, paper side up.

6 If your table is larger than the template, use the direct method to place pebble gray mosaics, face up, into some adhesive around the edges of the table to give it a neat border.

7 Wet the brown paper with a damp sponge and peel it off the mosaics; make sure you remove all of the paper. Then use an awl or similar tool to prick out any adhesive that has seeped over the edge of the mosaics—this would show through the grout if left in place. Wash the table with a damp sponge immediately afterwards.

8 Mix some gray grout and apply it using a grout float, making sure that you push the grout into all the gaps. When you have finished, remove the excess grout with a damp sponge and polish the table with a dry cloth. Allow to dry for 24 hours.

INSPIRATIONAL IDEAS

This versatile design could be used elsewhere in the home, perhaps as a backsplash on a kitchen wall or as decoration at the bottom of a Zen-style garden pond.

HINTS AND TIPS

- It is advisable to cut the brown paper to the exact size and shape needed before sticking on the tesserae.
- To free the tesserae from the sheets on which they are supplied, soak them in warm water; you'll find that this will dissolve the glue and they will then be ready to use.
- Read pages 7, 8, and 9 for information on cutting and mixing and advice on safety before starting this project.
- If your table is larger than the template but you do not want to add a border to the design, you could extend the lines to the outer edges of the table. You would either have to redraw the design to fit the table or complete the central section and then extend the lines of the design outward.
- If you are commissioning a new table for use outside, use marine plywood for the top and galvanized steel for the base.
- Paint the table legs black and varnish them to give a lacquer effect.

Moroccan-style geometric tabletop

TOOLS AND MATERIALS

Tracing paper

Gummed brown paper, or plain brown paper and gum glue

Pencil and ruler

Glass tesserae: ¾ x ¾in (2 x 2cm); quarter sheet of lime, one-and-a-half sheets of dark amethyst, three sheets of lilac, and one sheet of rich amethyst (for the border)

Tile cutters

Surgical and rubber gloves

Safety glasses and mask

PVA glue

Fine paintbrush

Craft knife

Plywood: 2ft (60cm) long x 2ft (60cm) wide x ½in (1cm) deep

Two buckets for mixing

Gray exterior powder adhesive and additive

Trowel

Notched trowel: ¼in (3mm)

Sponge

Awl or similar tool

Gray exterior powder grout and additive

Squeegee

Cloth

Metal table base

GLASS TESSERAE COLORS

Lime citrus

Dark amethyst

Soft lilac

Rich amethyst

The art of mosaic in Morocco has traditionally been passed down from father to son for many centuries. Religion dictates that design throughout Morocco depicts no living thing, so geometric design dominates all forms of decoration. For this reason, Moroccan mosaic makers have always been talented mathematicians as well as incredible craftsmen. This tabletop pattern is a stunning example of skilled geometry. The scale is designed to keep the cutting of tiles to a minimum, which makes this project extremely easy to make, and complementary shades of lilac and amethyst contrast effectively with a vibrant lime citrus. A plywood tabletop is used in conjunction with a simply constructed linear iron base; together they make the ideal setting for a Moroccan mint tea party.

Using the template

Trace the template at the back of the book, turn the tracing paper over, and draw over the outline on the reverse in pencil. Turn the tracing back over and position it on some brown paper. Trace over the front, transferring the design onto the paper.

1 Trace the design from the template onto brown paper. Use a ruler to ensure straight lines. You might find it useful to stick the template onto the paper with low-tack tape to stop it from moving around while you are tracing.

2 Turn over the brown paper and draw an unbroken line from left to right across the paper. By doing this, when you come to stick the mosaic onto the plywood, you will have clear registration marks to help you match up the four sections.

3 Cut the tesserae for the whole project. The lime citrus tiles need to be scored and snapped into triangles. The border is a combination of one row of whole tiles and one row of a half tiles, so cut some half tiles, too.

4 Using a damp sponge on gummed brown paper or gum glue on plain brown paper, stick the tiles face down onto the traced design. Work in sections. If your triangles are not 100 percent accurate, you may need to trim them carefully with tile cutters, shaving off any excess.

5 Once all the tiles are stuck in position, use a craft knife to cut the paper into quarters. Turn the sections over so they are still in the right position and make sure all the pencil lines on the reverse correspond with the original layout.

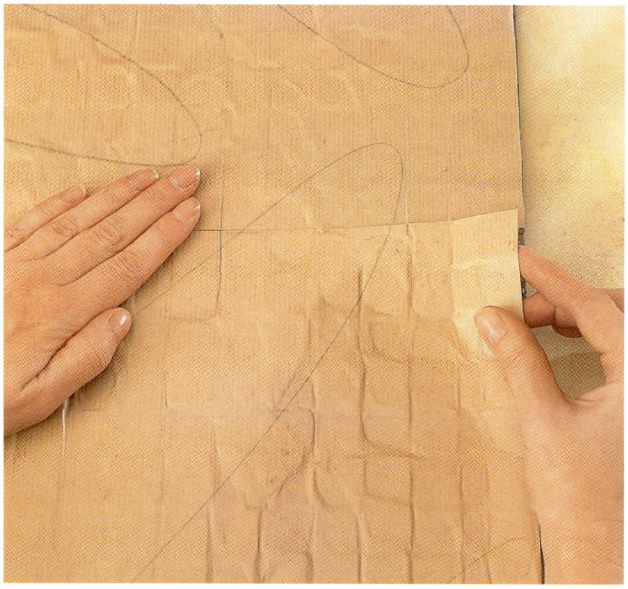

6 Prime the plywood with PVA glue and allow to dry. Then, using a notched trowel, apply adhesive. Position each section of the mosaic on the plywood, checking that the tiles do not hang over the edge.

7 Wet the back of the brown paper with a sponge and let the water soak in before peeling off the paper. Do not rush this process or the tiles will lift off with the paper; wait until it peels off easily. Some tiles may move slightly when the paper is removed—simply reposition these as you go. Prick out any excess adhesive from between the tesserae with an awl or similar tool.

8 Wearing protective gloves, mix some grout (see page 9). Spread it between the tiles using a squeegee to push the grout into all the spaces. Wipe off any excess grout and clean the surface with a damp sponge. A fine layer of residue will remain, but this will be cleaned off when you give the mosaic a final polish. With the aid of a friend, lift and lower the mosaic onto the metal table base.

HINTS AND TIPS

- Be sure to wear a filter mask when cutting tesserae to give protection against dust particles that can irritate your lungs.
- Dilute water-soluble PVA glue in a ratio of 3 parts glue to 2 parts water.
- Use a trowel to apply adhesive to large areas such as this repetitive geometric design.
- When removing the design from the brown paper, you may have to repeat the wetting process several times before the paper comes away easily.
- The wooden tabletop should be a fraction of an inch smaller than the metal frame to allow space for grout.

INSPIRATIONAL IDEAS

The base for this table was specially designed, but you could just as easily use an old iron table from a salvage yard. Simply drill a piece of plywood, cut it to fit the existing tabletop, and screw it in place. For outside use, cover the plywood with a protective coating.

Shell-effect baseboard

TOOLS AND MATERIALS

Sections of particle board (enough to cover your wall): 1ft (30cm) long x 9in (23cm) wide x ½in (1cm) deep

Medium-grit sandpaper and block

PVA glue

Paintbrush

Electric drill and countersink bit

Tracing paper

Pencil

Porcelain tiles: 4 x 4in (10 x 10cm); five of each color

Tile cutters

Surgical and rubber gloves

Safety glasses and mask

Mosaic nippers

Plain paper

Two buckets for mixing

Beige powder adhesive and additive

Trowel

Awl or similar tool

Beige powder grout and additive

Sponge

Cloth

Plastic wall anchors and screws

PORCELAIN TESSERAE COLORS

Rich burgundy

Deep olive

This elaborate and ancient pattern, found throughout Morocco, creates a delicate, lattice effect along the length of a baseboard. It appears complicated but is incredibly easy to create. The key to success is to cut plenty of small triangles before you start working on the design. The basic shell pattern is built up from glossy burgundy and dark green porcelain tiles, which are set off with a beige grout. The shiny, reflective surface of the tiles is enhanced by the matte finish of the grout. When your baseboard is complete and in place, you will find that the surface shines and glistens, picking up and reflecting light. It shimmers and sparkles. Do not feel limited to using this design just along a baseboard: it would work equally well decorating a picture frame or garden steps to evoke an exotic ambience.

Using the template

Trace the template at the back of the book, turn the tracing paper over, and draw over the outline on the reverse in pencil. Turn it back over and place it over the particle board. Trace over the front, transferring the design onto the board. You will need to reuse this template to create enough sections to cover the length of the baseboard.

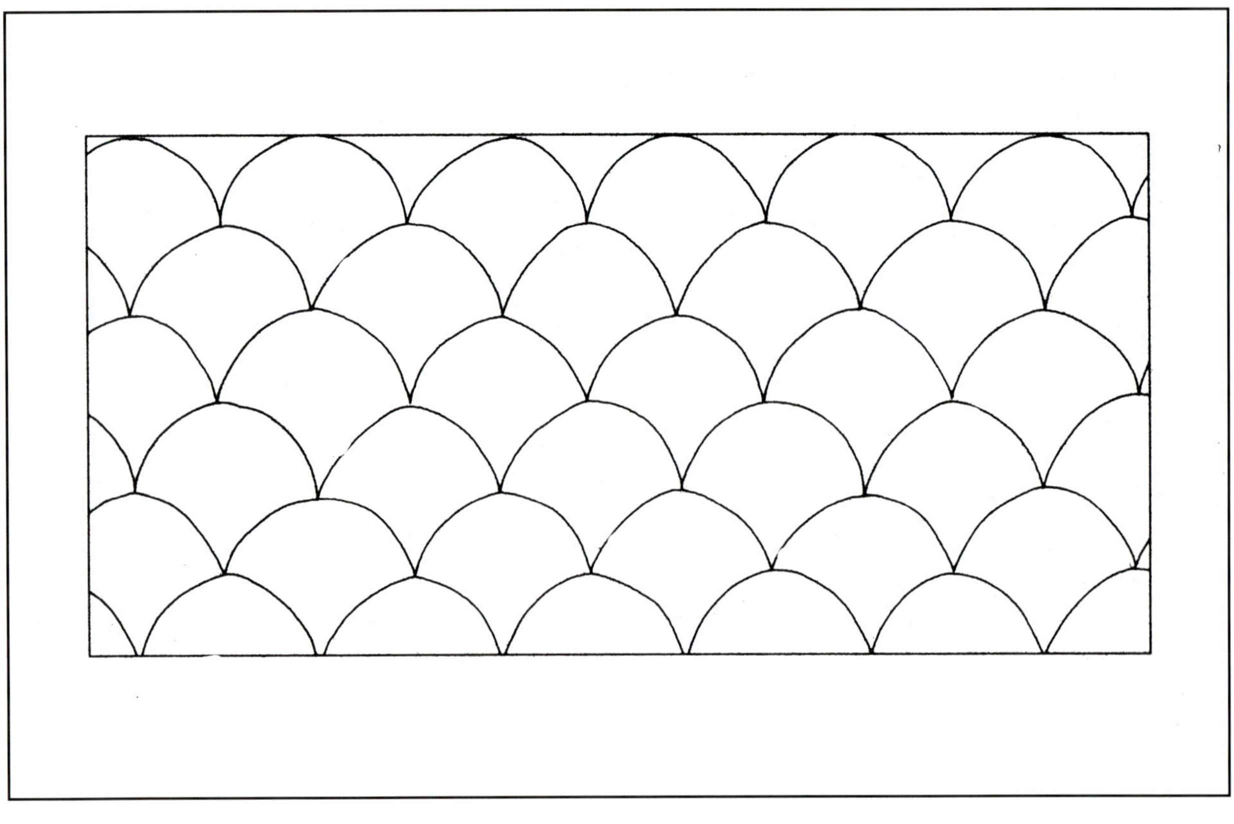

1 Take each section of wood and sand the edges. Apply two coats of PVA glue to the wood. Drill a hole in all four corners of each section of wood, then drill over the hole with a countersink bit. This will prevent the screws from protruding.

2 Trace the design from the template and transfer it onto each wood section using a pencil. Tracing onto a surface that has been covered with PVA can be difficult, so you may need to retrace the marks free-hand to make them easier to see.

3 Score lines along each tile using the blade of the tile cutters, then use the snapper part to break them into strips. Remember to wear protective goggles in case of flying splinters and a mask to stop the inhalation of tile dust.

4 Secure each strip between the blades of the mosaic nippers and cut at a 45° angle one way and 45° the other. This creates little V-shaped pieces with flat bottoms, ready to form the arches within the shell shape.

5 Draw a shell shape on a piece of paper and practice positioning the tesserae. This way you will know roughly how many pieces are required for each arch. This is not a precise science and each section must be treated as a separate space.

6 Mix a quantity of adhesive (see page 9) and trowel it neatly onto one shell shape. Position the tesserae, piece by piece, beginning at the top of the shell. This way you work in arches from top to bottom. It is important that there are the same number of rows and a single piece at the bottom of each shell shape.

7 To complete the project, work in rows of shell shapes, color by color, from top to bottom. Take it slowly and calmly, working methodically in one direction. Remember to leave drill holes uncovered. Allow to dry for 24 hours before pricking out the excess adhesive with an awl or similar tool.

8 Mix some grout (see page 9) and trowel it into the gaps. Clean off the excess with a damp sponge. Wearing protective gloves, smooth the grout with your fingers over the top edge of the baseboard so that the wood is covered and it is slightly domed: this adds to the rustic, Moroccan look. Allow the grout to dry for 24 hours. For attaching the mosaic to the wall, see Hints and Tips (below).

HINTS AND TIPS

- Tile cutters are the best tool for cutting tiles of this size, as they score a guideline before making the cut. Scoring weakens the tile so that it breaks exactly where you want and not randomly at an angle.
- You will need to prepare many more tesserae than you might think for this project—the edges of most tiles are slightly beveled making them unsuitable for this pattern, so there will be some wastage.
- Once your grout is dry, fix the mosaic to the wall. With an electric drill, drill holes in the wall in the same position as those in the mosaic and fit plastic wall anchors, then screw the mosaic in place. Mix a small amount of adhesive and stick the tesserae over the area covering the screws. Allow to dry for 24 hours. Prick out excess adhesive with an awl, grout, wipe clean, and polish.

INSPIRATIONAL IDEAS

This pattern lends itself to experimentation with different color combinations. Creating each shell shape in a different color scheme would produce a vibrant and very modern mosaic. This design would work well for a floor mosaic—just reuse the template to create a repeating pattern.

KITCHENS & BATHROOMS

Greek key design bathmat

TOOLS AND MATERIALS

Glass tesserae: ¾ x ¾ in (2 x 2cm)

Exterior-grade particle board: 33in (84cm) long x 15 in (39.5cm) wide x 1in (2.5cm) deep

Waterproof PVA glue

Paintbrush

Gummed brown paper, or plain brown paper and gum glue

Pencil, ruler, and tracing paper

Surgical and rubber gloves

Mask

Fine paintbrush

Two buckets for mixing

White exterior powder adhesive

White exterior powder grout

Notched trowel: ⅛ in (3mm)

Palette knife

Sponge

Awl or similar tool

GLASS TESSERAE COLORS

Deep aqua

Mid aqua

Pale aqua

The key motif is one of the most instantly recognizable Greek designs. Its simple, repeating pattern runs in a continuous, seemingly endless line. The key was typically used as an edging for elaborate designs on pottery and chiseled into sculptures, as well as featuring as a detail on clothing and jewelry. Throughout ancient and modern Greece, it appears widely—on ornaments in the home, on the surrounding magnificent architecture, and even as a linear border on traditional Greek costumes. This project is simple to make because there is no cutting of tesserae involved, and the indirect method is used to apply the tiles to the wooden base of the bathmat. The combination of pale blues and aqua sets the scene for a peaceful, tranquil refuge in your bathroom.

Using the template

Trace the template at the back of the book, turn the tracing paper over, and draw over the outline on the reverse in pencil. Turn the tracing back over and position it on the brown paper. Trace over the front, transferring the design onto the brown paper. For this particular design, it helps to shade in the pattern so that you can see clearly where the tesserae should be positioned. They are applied using the indirect method (see page 11 for instructions).

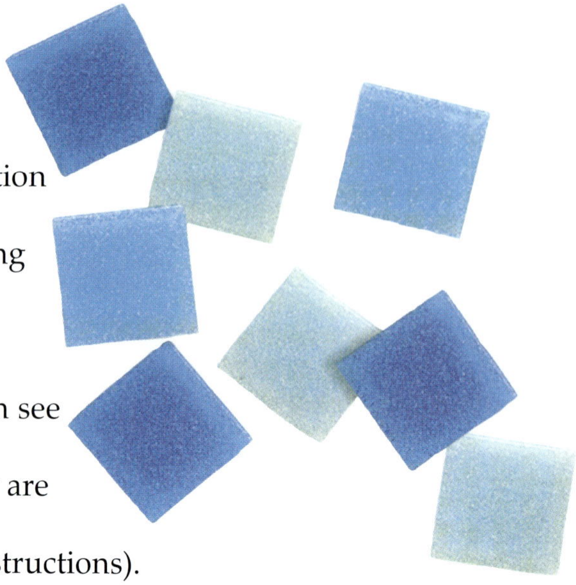

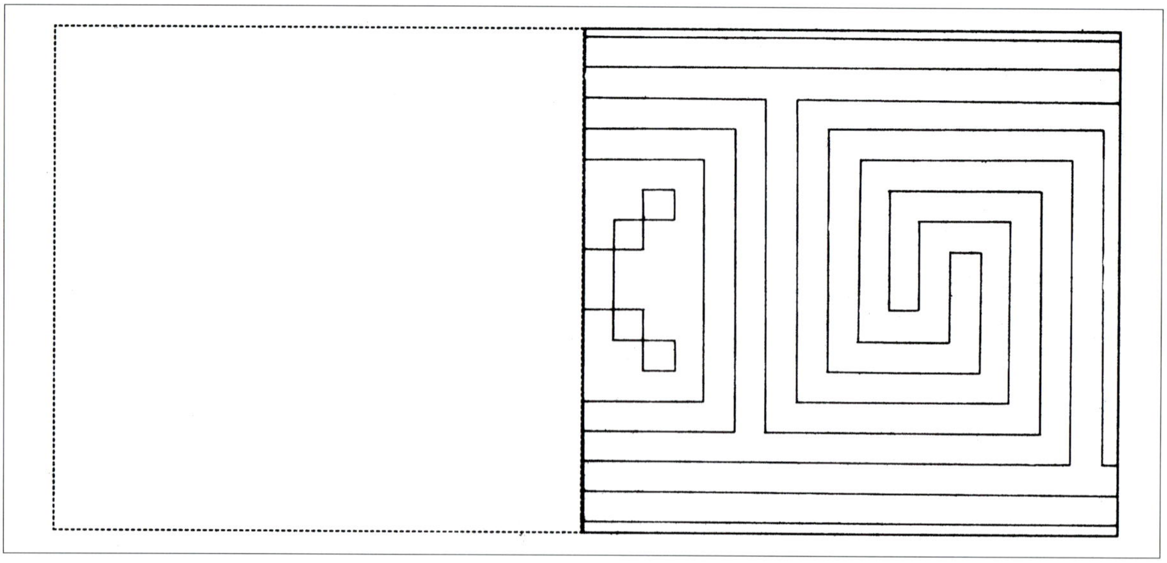

1 First, paint the front, back, and sides of the wood with two coats of waterproof PVA glue to seal it. This is essential if you are going to use the mat in a bathroom or it will eventually absorb water, expand, and start to disintegrate, even if you have used exterior-grade wood.

2 Transfer the template onto the brown paper (see instructions on page 36). You will now have a faint linear image on the brown paper. Using a pencil, shade in the pattern so that it will be easy to where the tesserae should be positioned.

3 Using a damp sponge on gummed brown paper or gum glue on plain brown paper, stick the tesserae into position face down. Try to keep the gaps between the tiles equal so that the grout will look regular and even.

4 Now fill in the background color so the design is complete and you are ready to stick the tiles to the wood. Turn the paper over and draw a few lines across the back. Cut the pattern in half with a craft knife so that you have two smaller sections—these will be easier to maneuve. The lines you drew on the back will enable you to align the two pattern pieces accurately when you put them in position on the particle board base.

5 Apply adhesive to the wood using a notched trowel and gently lower each half of the design into place. Next, using a small trowel, apply adhesive onto the backs of the darkest tesserae and stick them one by one onto the edges of the board, being careful not to disturb the pattern.

6 Allow to dry for 24 hours. Wet the brown paper with a damp sponge and wait for it to soak in. The paper should peel off easily in two sections. If any tiles come loose, stick them down again.

7 Wait for the adhesive to dry. Some of it might seep through and stick out above the tiles. Using an awl or similar tool to prick out the excess, then dust away the dry adhesive. You are now ready to grout.

HINTS AND TIPS

- If this is your first attempt, draw a rough sketch of the grid to help you position the tiles.
- Don't try to peel off the paper too soon—it takes longer to dry than you might think.
- You may want to stick on rubber feet to raise the bathmat off the ground slightly so that water has less chance to seep in.
- You could use a wooden molding as edging instead of tiles.

8 Mix the grout and spread it over the whole mosaic. Disperse it with a squeegee or trowel, and work it into the gaps. Use your fingers to neaten the grout around the outside of the design. You may need to wait for the outside edges to dry and regrout to get a good edge. Polish the mosaic with a cloth and the project is complete.

INSPIRATIONAL IDEAS

By using quarter tiles you can shrink the design to make a pretty border running along the top of a baseboard or at chair rail height, or an attractive surround for a mirror.

Vibrant star water bowl

TOOLS AND MATERIALS

Flat-bottomed terra-cotta bowl: 16in (40cm) diameter

Waterproof PVA glue

Paintbrush

Tracing paper

Gummed brown paper, or plain brown paper and gum glue

Pencil and scissors

Glass tesserae: ¾ x ¾ in (2 x 2cm); one sheet of red, half sheet of black and deep orange, and three-quarter sheet of tangerine orange

Tile cutters

Surgical and rubber gloves

Safety glasses and mask

Fine paintbrush

Two buckets for mixing

Black exterior powder adhesive and additive

Notched trowel: ¼ in (3mm)

Trowel

Sponge

Awl or similar tool tool

Masking tape

Black exterior powder grout and additive

Squeegee

Cloth

GLASS TESSERAE COLORS

Jet black

Tangerine orange

Deep orange

Blood red

Decorate a plain bowl with intensely colored glass tesserae, in a palette that evokes the exotic spice markets of Marrakesh. The intricate design works harmoniously with the bright hues, whereas the contrasting black grout highlights the colors. Although the pattern is quite complicated, if you tackle small sections at a time it is easily achieved, and as the overall project is quite small, it does not take long to complete. To relax away from the bustle of everyday life, Moroccans often sit in the sanctuary of cool courtyards and float aromatic rose petals and flowers in their fountains. Emulate this custom by filling this stunning bowl with water and floating your own choice of blooms. Or you might prefer to float scented candles across the surface to set the scene for a candlelit Moroccan dinner.

Using the template

Trace the template at the back of the book, turn the tracing paper over, and draw over the outline on the reverse in pencil. Turn the tracing back over and position it on brown paper. Trace over the front, transferring the design onto the brown paper. Cut out the bowl shape, so that it fits inside the bowl.

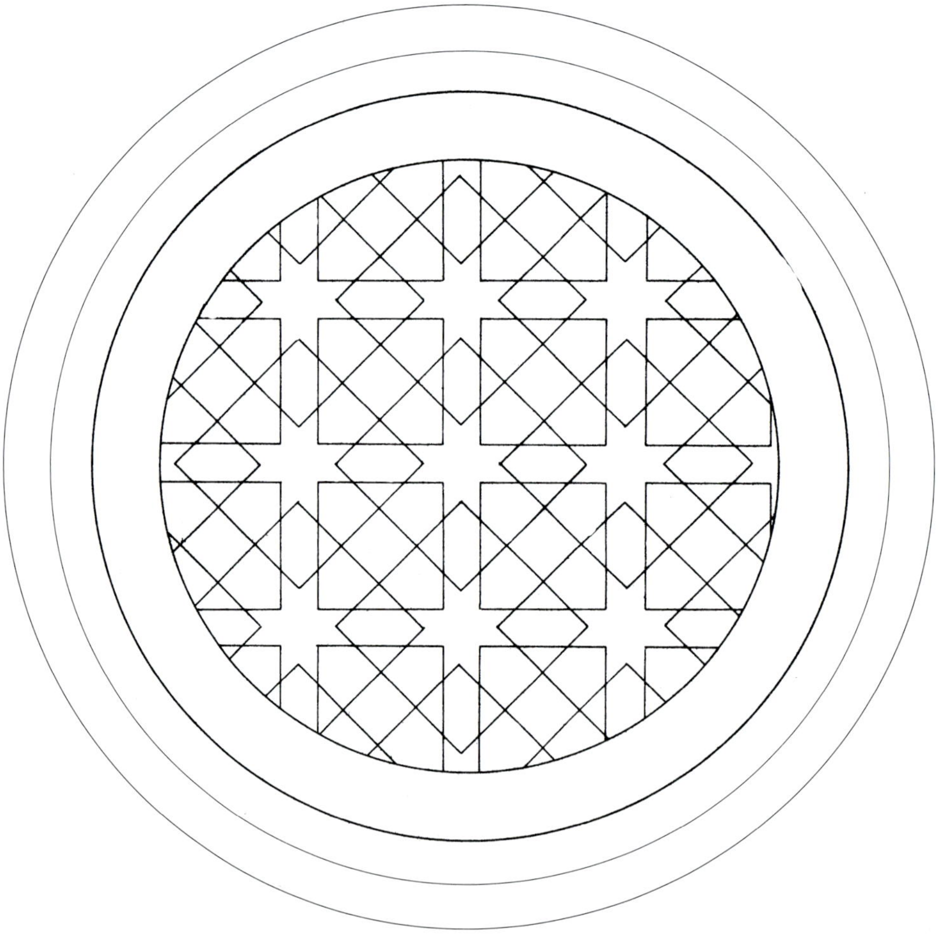

1 Give the terra-cotta bowl two coats of PVA glue, inside and out, to make it water-resistant. Terra-cotta is very porous, so test how watertight the bowl is by filling it with water and leaving it on the side of a sink to see if the water seeps through.

2 Trace the template from the back of the book and transfer it onto brown paper. Using tile cutters, cut the tiles into strips, squares, and triangles (see page 8). Lay out the tesserae on the pattern before you start gluing, as this is a complicated design.

3 Each space of this design requires a different cut of tesserae and so there is a lot of nipping, scoring, and snapping to do. You may find cutting tricky at first but it does become easier as you proceed. Then, using a damp sponge on gummed brown paper or gum glue on plain brown paper, stick the tesserae into position face down. Complete the pattern and allow them to dry.

4 Mix a quantity of adhesive and smear it on the base of the bowl using the flat side of the trowel—if any sticks to the upright edge, clean it off. Smooth the surface evenly, then use the notched side of the trowel to make grooves in it.

5 Carefully lower the entire circle onto the adhesive, butting it up to the edges. Once the whole circle is down, gently wiggle the tiles into the adhesive to make sure they are grounded. Put aside for 24 hours to allow the adhesive to set.

6 Wet the paper with a sponge and gently peel it away from the tiles (you may need to keep wetting the paper). Some tiles may stay on the paper—peel them off and stick them on separately.

7 To mosaic the upright edge, apply adhesive to whole red tiles and push them into place. Make sure there is a gap surrounding each tile for the grout, and that they are spaced as evenly as possible. When the circle is nearly complete, you may need to readjust the spacing between each tile (use only whole tiles). Prick out any excess adhesive from between the tesserae with a bradawl.

8 Stick pieces of masking tape along the top edge of the bowl to make a neat circle. Mix some grout and apply it to the bottom of the bowl and up the sides with a squeegee. Take the grout up to the masked edge and smooth it neatly. When the grout is almost dry, peel off the tape to reveal a neat edge. Allow the grout to set for 24 hours, then polish with a dry cloth.

HINTS AND TIPS

- Because there are many different shapes in this design and you do not want to waste tiles through miscutting, follow the instructions on page 8 for Cutting and Scoring.
- It is advisable to cut all the tesserae before you start to lay them so that you do not have to break off mid-flow.
- Work in small sections when grouting your mosaic. This will enable you to wipe away any excess before it dries hard.
- If you are planning to fill this bowl with water, do not place it directly on a treasured piece of furniture the first time in case any liquid seeps through.

INSPIRATIONAL IDEAS

The vivid color combination chosen for this bowl is typically Moroccan. This intricate design would work in any colour scheme: blues and greens would be especially effective. Remember to use a grout that matches your colors.

Urn & vines backsplash

TOOLS AND MATERIALS

Tape measure
Level
Pencil
Tracing paper
Waterproof PVA glue and paintbrush
Vitreous glass tesserae: ¾ x ¾ in (2 x 2cm)
Mosaic nippers
Surgical and rubber gloves
Safety glasses and mask
Adhesive and additive
Two buckets for mixing
Palette knife
Trowel
Notched trowel: ¼ in (3mm)
Awl or similar tool
Beige and white powder grout and additive
Grout float or rubber squeegee
Drop cloth
Sponge
Soft cloth

GLASS TESSERAE COLORS

Butterscotch
Caramel
Toffee
Amethyst
Lilac
Grass green
Mint green
Olive with gold vein
Gray green
Charcoal

What could be more stylish in your kitchen than a classical urn that is overflowing with fruits of the vine? While the design is truly Roman, the stylized form, bright colors, and use of glass tesserae give this project a contemporary feel. To provide extra sparkle in this backsplash, the leaves are made from glass tesserae that are marbled with gold leaf. A subtle tone of grout was used for this project to help the details to stand out. Although this mosaic looks elaborate, it is not difficult to make—you can cut most of the glass tesserae into irregular pieces of any shape. You will need to take a little extra care when making the delicate lines of the stalks, which require small tesserae, and the grapes, which need circular pieces.

Using the template

Trace the template at the back of the book, turn the tracing paper over, and draw over the outline on the reverse in pencil. Turn it back over and hold it against the wall. Trace over the front, transferring your design onto the wall. To create extra leaves, simply reuse the leaf on the template by moving the template around the wall and retracing the design.

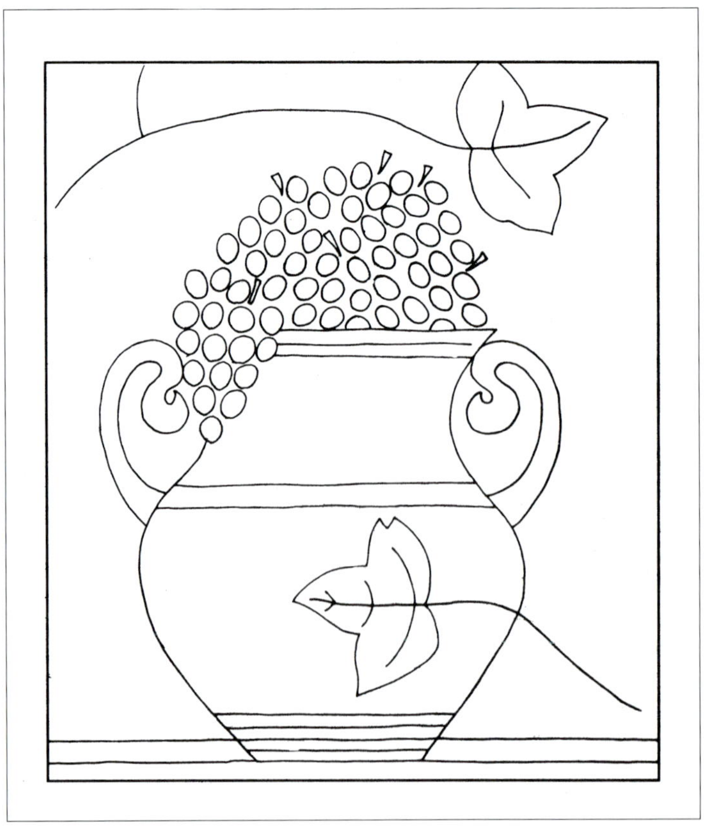

1 Using a tape measure and level, measure the width of the wall. With a pencil, make a small mark halfway across. Measure the height of the area, making another mark exactly halfway. Where these two marks meet is your center point.

2 Trace the template onto the wall (see Using the Template on page 60). Make sure that you line it up with the center point.

3 Prime the wall with two coats of waterproof PVA glue. While waiting for the glue to dry, start cutting the glass tesserae with mosaic nippers (see page 8). Always wear surgical gloves, safety glasses, and a mask when cutting vitreous glass.

4 Start with the grape area first. Mix some adhesive (see page 9) and apply a small amount to the grape area. Position the grapes firmly into the adhesive. Be sure to wear surgical gloves in order to protect your hands.

5 Next, work on the leaves. Use a palette knife to apply a small amount of adhesive to the area within the outline. Position the tesserae into the adhesive—work first on the stem, then the veins, and finally the rest of the leaves.

6 If you do not want to cover the pencil guidelines with the adhesive, you could apply adhesive to the back of each tessera and stick them on individually. This method is more time-consuming but will help while you are building up your confidence. Still wearing your surgical gloves, apply small mosaic squares to form the outline of the urn. Once this is complete, start filling in the urn with a random arrangement of mosaics—known as the "Opus Palladianum" method, this style of mosaicing is similar to the random pattern of crazy paving.

7 Once the details are complete, start on the background. Use a trowel to apply the adhesive to the wall, then groove the surface with a notched trowel. Position the tesserae, again using the "Opus Palladianum" method (see step 6).

8 Complete the effect by mosaicing a charcoal border above and below the design. Allow the mosaic to dry for 24 hours. Then, using an awl or similar tool, carefully remove any excess adhesive or it will show through the grout.

9 Mix the grout until you achieve a medium-thick consistency. The grout that was used for this project was made from 1 part beige powder grout to 3 parts white grout: this creates a subtle tone that matches the color of the background tesserae. Cover the surrounding area with a drop cloth because grouting can be messy. Wear rubber gloves to protect your hands and apply the grout using a float or squeegee. Push the grout firmly into the gaps between the tesserae and remove the excess with the squeegee.

10 Still wearing rubber gloves sponge off the excess grout. Constantly rinse your sponge in clean water, so that you do not smear the surface. Allow to dry, then polish the mosaic using a dry, soft cloth.

INSPIRATIONAL IDEAS

Try this design in different colors. The rich brown urn would look stylish against a sky blue background, while the grapes could be made with green and black tesserae. If you prefer, you could try filling the urn with other varieties of fruit. Blood-red pomegranates were a favorite of the Romans, while lemons and limes are typical Mediterranean fruits.

BEDROOMS & ACCESSORIES

Japanese screen

TOOLS AND MATERIALS

Vitreous glass tesserae: ¾ x ¾in (2 x 2cm)

Surgical and rubber gloves

Pencil

Margin trowel and trowel

Awl or similar tool

Grout float

Gummed brown paper, or plain brown paper and gum glue: 21in (54cm) long x 11in (28cm) wide

Notched trowel: ¼in (3mm)

Three particle board panels: 72in (183cm) long x 20in (50cm) wide x ⅛in (3mm) deep; each panel should have a rectangle grooved out: 21in (54cm) long x 11in (28cm) wide x ⅕in (5mm) deep

Six hinges to attach the panels

Tape measure and tracing paper

PVA glue and paintbrush

Mosaic nippers

Safety glasses and mask

White powder adhesive and additive

Two buckets for mixing

Palette knife

White powder grout and additive

Drop cloth, sponge, and cloth

GLASS TESSERAE COLORS

Bronze

Shiny black

Charcoal

Jade

Sharp white

Misty white

Brighter white

Screens have always played an important role in the Japanese home, whether they have been designed to divide, conceal, or protect. Traditionally, they are beautifully decorated with recognizable symbols, like the crane featured here, which was inspired by a Japanese screen painted in 1566. Cranes were commonly seen on objects d'art and 19th-century textiles. In Japan, cranes symbolize longevity and are also said to aid communication with the Divinities. The whiteness of the crane has been set on a jade green background. Vitreous glass mosaics offer a wide color range, and thus texture and tone can be given to the crane's feathers with the various shades of white tesserae. To finish the screen, it was painted black and varnished to give it a lacquered feel.

Using the template

Central panel: trace the template at the back of the book, turn over the tracing paper, and draw over the outline on the reverse in pencil. Turn it back over and place it on top of the brown paper. Trace over the front, transferring the design onto the brown paper. First and last panel: a template is not needed for these two panels because they consist of randomly cut pieces of jade mosaic with no pattern.

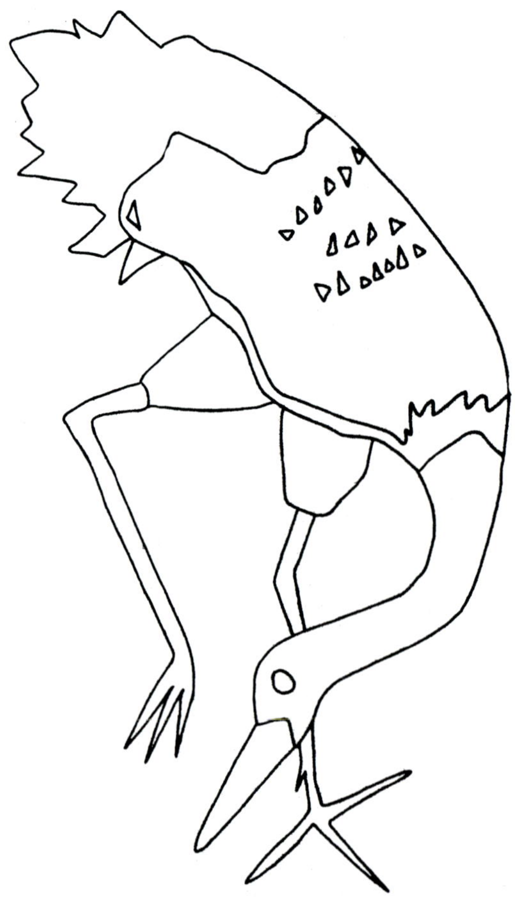

1 Remove any rough edges from the particle board with sandpaper and a block. Then seal with PVA glue. Allow to dry. Wearing rubber gloves, mix some powder adhesive and apply to a portion of one panel with a margin trowel.

2 Groove the surface of the adhesive with a notched trowel. Cut the sage green mosaics in random shapes using mosaic nippers. Stick the tesserae into the adhesive bed, keeping the spaces between them equal. Repeat over first and last panels.

3 Central panel: follow the template instructions as explained on page 70. Trace the design onto some brown paper. It is a good idea to draw over the pencil outline of the crane in black felt-tip pen—this makes it easier to follow when you start sticking down the tiles. Secure the template to your base with masking tape while you are tracing the image, to help keep it in place. Once you have completed the design, cut all the colored tesserae pieces you will need to complete the crane.

4 Central panel: using a damp sponge on gummed brown paper or gum glue on plain brown paper, stick the tesserae into position smooth side down. Complete the detail of the bird, then the jade background. Allow to dry.

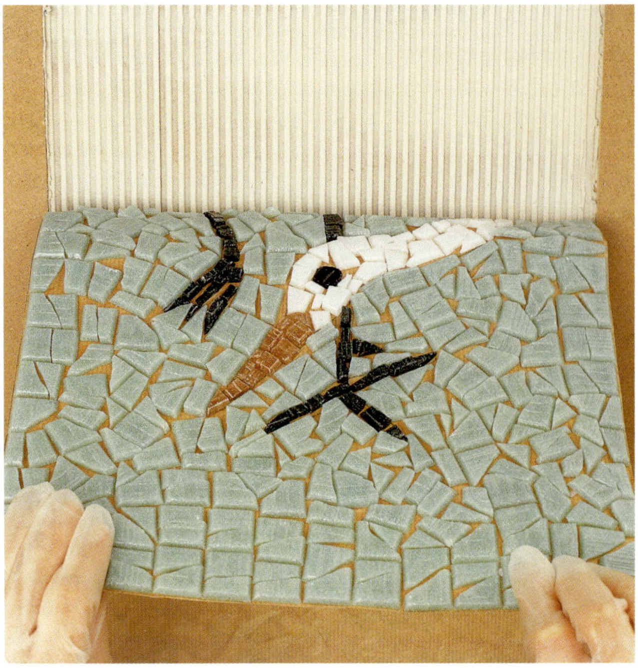

5 Central panel: mix some adhesive and apply it to the central panel, then groove it with the notched trowel. Carefully place the mosaic, paper side up, into the bed of adhesive. Allow it to dry for 24 hours.

6 Central panel: wet the brown paper using a damp sponge and gently peel it away. Make sure you remove all traces of the paper.

7 Central, first, and last panels: clean the mosaic with a sponge and prick out any unwanted lumps of adhesive with an awl or similar tool. Work on one panel at a time. Wash the panels with a damp sponge afterwards.

8 Central, first, and last panels: mix some white grout and apply using a grout float. Remove excess grout with a damp sponge and polish with a dry cloth. Work on one panel at a time.

HINTS AND TIPS

Paint the screen with black latex, wait for it to dry, then varnish using clear marine varnish.

- A carpenter made the screen featured here. The positioning of the hinges determines the direction or angle of movement of the screen. You must decide how you want it to stand and inform your carpenter.
- It is advisable to cut the brown paper to the exact size and shape needed before sticking on the tesserae.
- To free the tesserae from their backing, leave them to soak in warm water, which will dissolve the glue; they will then be ready to use.

INSPIRATIONAL IDEAS

The bird design could be applied onto some marine plywood, 21in (54cm) long x 11in (28cm) wide, and used as a decorative wall plaque in a garden.

Chinese photo album

TOOLS AND MATERIALS

Electric drill and countersink bit

Two pieces of plywood: 16in (40cm) long x 12in (30cm) wide x 4mm (⅛ in) deep

Black latex paint

Clear marine varnish

Paintbrush

Pencil

Ruler

Vitreous glass tesserae: ¾ x ¾ in (2 x 2cm)

Gummed brown paper, or plain brown paper and gum glue, for circular motif

Surgical and rubber gloves

Sponge and cloth

Tape measure

Leather strap

Recycled paper and rice paper

PVA glue

Mosaic nippers

Safety glasses and mask

White powder adhesive and additive

Two buckets for mixing

Notched trowel: ¼ in (3mm)

Trowel

Awl or similar tool

White powder grout and additive

Hole punch

Tracing paper

GLASS TESSERAE COLORS

1lb (0.5kg) gold leaf mosaic—smooth surface

Charcoal

White

This decorative Chinese photograph album would make an ideal gift or an excellent ornament. The simple color scheme of white, black, and gold creates a stylish look with a touch of wealth. The Chinese symbol used here means "Riches," which could apply to the beautiful handmade album itself as well as the photographs it contains, with all their happy memories. To make the album really special, you could add a leather strap for the tie and place some recycled paper inside, which you can either buy or make yourself. Thick, handmade paper with red rose petals sprinkled on a white background was used here. Rice paper was cut and inserted between each sheet of handmade paper to protect the photographs, which can be attached with adhesive corner mounts.

Using the template

For Board 2, the front of the album, you should make the circular motif separately on brown paper. Trace the template at the back of the book, turn the tracing paper over, and draw over the outline on the reverse in pencil. Turn it back over and place it on top of brown paper. Trace the lines again, transferring the design onto the brown paper. Once the black border has been laid, you will apply tesserae directly to complete the background—no template is required for this area. For Board 1 (the back of the album), use the template to draw the black border, then apply the tesserae directly onto the rest of the surface.

1 Drill two pilot holes through both boards at 2in (5cm) from the width of the board and 4in (10cm) away from the top/length. Remove the rough edges with sandpaper and a block. Then apply PVA glue to the front on the boards. Allow to dry.

2 Paint the back of both boards using black latex paint. Allow to dry, then varnish with clear yacht varnish. Cut the white mosaic in random shapes and the gold leaf in small oblong shapes, but leave the black mosaic on the sheets.

3 On the front of both boards, measure in 4in (10.5cm) from the outside edge. Mark a line at this level, showing where the division between the white and black mosaic should lie.

4 Boards 1 and 2: mix some adhesive and apply it where the black mosaic will be. Groove the surface with a notched trowel, then place the mosaic smooth side up into the adhesive. Remove any tesserae that block the drilled holes.

5 Boards 1 and 2: remove any brown paper from the black tesserae by soaking them in warm water. Cut the mosaic to fit around the holes, making sure that you wear safety glasses when cutting. Place the mosaics into the adhesive.

6 Board 2 (front of album): detach the template from the back of the book, trace the Chinese motif, and transfer the design onto some brown paper (see the instructions on page 74). Using a damp sponge on gummed brown paper or gum glue on plain brown paper, stick the tesserae (the gold leaf and white mosaic) into position smooth side down. Complete the pattern and allow them to dry.

7 Board 2 (front of album): mix some adhesive and apply to the board. Groove the surface of the adhesive with a notched trowel. Position the Chinese motif, paper side up, on top of the adhesive, making sure it is central. Then start sticking the white tesserae, smooth side up, directly into the adhesive. Fit the tesserae together like a jigsaw puzzle. If there are any gaps, you may need to cut exact pieces to fit. Allow to dry for 24 hours. On Board 1 (back of album), position white mosaics into the adhesive, smooth side up. Work around the symbol moving outward until you have reached the edge of the album.

8 Board 2 (front of album): take a damp sponge and wet the paper before peeling back to reveal the motif. Use a bradawl to prick out any unwanted adhesive.

9 Mix some grout and apply it to Boards 1 and 2 using a grout float. Remove excess grout with a damp sponge and polish. Allow to dry for 24 hours.

INSPIRATIONAL IDEAS

This motif has such a beautiful appearance and meaning that it would make a wonderful wall plaque or a picture. You could find other Chinese symbols that appeal to you and create other mosaic projects.

HINTS AND TIPS

- It is advisable to cut the brown paper to the exact size and shape needed before sticking on the tesserae.
- To free the tesserae from their backing, leave them to soak in warm water, which will dissolve the glue; they will then be ready to use.
- Always read the advice given on cutting, safety, and mixing on pages 7, 8, and 9.
- After using PVA glue, wash your paintbrush immediately with soapy water.
- Remove excess varnish from your paint-brush following the instructions given by manufacturer.
- You will need to cut the handmade and rice paper sheets to size and punch holes in them in the correct positions to match the outer shell of the album.

Gilded minaret mirror

TOOLS AND MATERIALS

- Two pieces of particle board: 2ft (60cm) long x 11in (28cm) wide x ½in (1cm) deep
- Pencil and ruler
- Jigsaw
- Tracing paper
- Electric drill
- PVA glue
- Paintbrush
- C-clamps or heavy weights
- Tesserae: ¾ x ¾in (2 x 2cm); two sheets of blue glass and 100 gold leaf tesserae
- Mosaic nippers
- Tile cutters
- Surgical and rubber gloves
- Safety glasses and mask
- Two buckets for mixing
- Gray powder adhesive and additive
- Trowel
- Fine paintbrush
- Sandpaper and block
- Awl or similar tool
- Gray powder grout and additive
- Squeegee
- Sponge
- Cloth
- Mirror: 1½ft x 7½in (47 x 19cm)
- Hardboard: 1½ft x 7½in (47 x 19cm)
- Finish nails and hammer

TESSERAE COLORS

- Midnight blue with gold fleck
- Gold leaf

This exquisite mirror combines a bold architectural outline with a delicate and intricate design. The result is an authentic-looking product of North Africa. The undulating design is reminiscent of Arabic script, but with an organic essence, as it twists and twines its way around the frame. Although this is one of the more complicated projects in the book, it is relatively easy once you get started, so do not be afraid to take on the challenge. Once you have mastered the scoring and snapping of the tiles, it will be plain sailing. Whether resting on a mantelpiece in bright sunshine or illuminated by candles at night, this mirror, with its midnight blue and gold leaf glass, will conjure up the atmosphere, magic, and mystery of the Arabian Nights.

Using the template

Trace the template at the back of the book, turn the tracing paper over, and draw over the outline on the reverse in pencil. Turn the tracing back over and place it on the first piece of particle board. Trace the border design over the front, transferring the design onto the particle board. Lift the tracing off and place it on the second piece of particle board and repeat, tracing the minaret shape.

1 To make the mirror frame, take one piece of particle board and measure 1½in (4cm) in from the bottom and sides. Make several marks along these edges. Along the top, measure in 2in (8cm) and make marks. Join up all the marks to form a rectangle. Use a jigsaw to cut out this shape.

2 Using the template at the back of the book, trace the outline of the minaret onto the second piece of wood. Be sure to center the design. Remember to use a soft pencil for the reverse tracing as it will maximize the carbon on the back and give a stronger traced line.

3 Drill a hole in the second piece of particle board, insert the jigsaw, and cut out the minaret. Cut the straight lines first, then guide the jigsaw gently around the curves. You may have to drill extra holes to get into tight corners. Do not push the jigsaw to speed up this part of the process—the particle board will cut easily if you let the jigsaw proceed at its own pace.

4 Squeeze a good quantity of strong PVA glue onto the back of the second piece of particle board (the minaret shape), keeping within the confines of the border. Clamp the two pieces of particle board together, or position a heavy object on top, and allow to dry. With a paintbrush, apply a layer of PVA glue as a sealant. Allow to dry until the glue is transparent.

5 Using mosaic nippers, cut the blue glass tiles into halves and then quarters. You will need these for the inside edge of the mirror. It doesn't matter if the shapes are irregular or if the tiles shatter. This design can accommodate a variety of irregular shapes. Cut lots of small triangles at different angles. Keep all the bits that splinter off as they will always find a home somewhere.

6 Score and snap the gold leaf tesserae with tile cutters, using the method described on page 8. To make tiny triangles, score the tesserae from corner to corner and then snap. Insert only around a quarter of the tesserae into the cutters, using the scored line as a central guide. Apply gentle pressure and the tesserae should snap easily, with minimal shattering. Continue dividing the triangles until they are small enough. For the tiny rectangles, divide the tiles in half before scoring and snapping. Use the nippers to create little pieces. You should be able to get four small pieces from one half.

7 Mix a small quantity of adhesive (see page 9). Starting on the outside edge, apply adhesive to whole tiles and hold each one in position for a couple of seconds. Work your way around the whole frame. If, when you are nearing an edge, it becomes clear that a gap is too small for a whole tile, add a half tile somewhere along the line.

8 Using either halves or quarters, move on to the inside edge of the minaret. The straight edges are easy and the curves are slightly trickier. Apply adhesive to each mosaic piece as before and hold in place. Allow to dry for at least three hours before starting the main design.

9 Trace the curly pattern onto the mirror frame. Mix a quantity of runny adhesive and use a fine paintbrush to apply it to the tracing. Do this in lines and work quickly before it dries. If you are too optimistic and the adhesive dries before you get there, sand it off and start again.

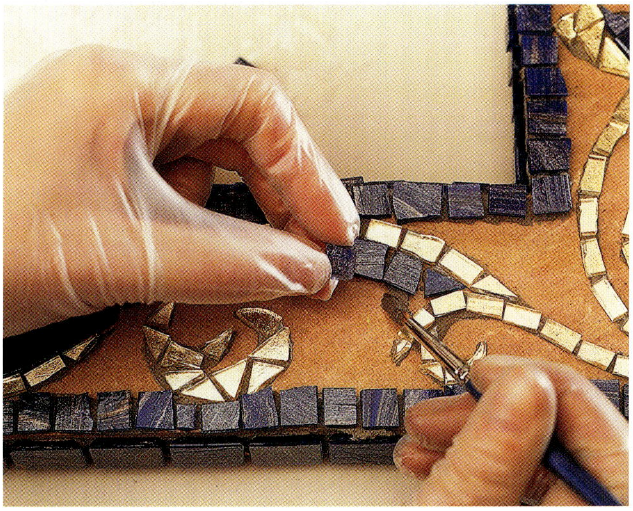

10 Fill in the background with quarter blue tiles, working in lines against the gold curves to give them the illusion of movement. You will need a lot of irregular pieces and triangles to fill in all the gaps. Allow to dry for 24 hours before pricking out the excess adhesive with an awl or similar tool. Mix some grout (see page 9) and spread it over the design with a squeegee, pushing it into the gaps. Wipe away excess with a damp sponge. Allow to dry for 24 hours and polish with a cloth. See Hints and Tips for hanging the mirror.

HINTS AND TIPS

- When tracing the curly pattern onto the mirror frame, you may need to draw over the outline again because the PVA glue is a difficult surface to mark with pencil.
- If the adhesive outline dries before you get a chance to cover it with gold tesserae, simply rub it off with sandpaper and start the outline again.
- Set yourself a small section to complete at a time—do not try to mosaic too much in one go; it will probably take a few sittings to finish.
- To attach the mirror into the frame, first paint the back of the frame black, paying special attention to the edges of the minaret. Slot in the mirror and hardboard backing. Then secure with nails, gently hammering them into the side of the frame so that they prevent the mirror and backing from falling out.

INSPIRATIONAL IDEAS

For a glamorous interior, the curly gold design could be used as a baseboard and continued around the door casing.

GARDENS & OUTDOORS

Zen garden wall tiles

TOOLS AND MATERIALS

Polished marble tesserae: 5/8 x 5/8 in (1.5 x 1.5cm)
PVA glue and paintbrush
Surgical and rubber gloves
Scissors
Awl or similar tool
Six pieces of marine plywood: 8in (20cm) long x 8hn (20cm) wide x 3/4 in (2cm) deep
Sponge
White powder grout and additive
Notched trowel: 1/4 in (3mm)
Trowel
Cloth
Safety glasses and mask
Marble protector
Color enhancer
Marble impregnator
Craft knife
Sandpaper and block
White powder adhesive and additive
Two buckets for mixing
Grout float
Paintbrush and white latex (or a color of your choice)
Tracing paper and pencil
Clear marine varnish

MARBLE TESSERAE COLORS

Black
White with gray flecks
Green
Terra-cotta
Cream

Create a Zen feel in your garden by adding these simple, yet stylish, garden tiles to any wall. Their refined design is a great backdrop for relaxation and calm. In the Chinese and Japanese school of Mahayana Buddhism, it is believed that enlightenment can be attained through the practice of reflection and meditation. Add the tiles to a peaceful corner of your garden to complement a relaxed seating area with a screen of Asian bamboo. This is an ideal first project for beginners as there is no cutting involved. The color scheme used here features marble mosaics in black, cream, green, terra-cotta, and white with gray flecks. The marble has been polished to add to the elegant look. Feel free to experiment and create your own tiles by using different mosaic colors or a different design.

Using the template

Trace the template at the back of the book, turn the tracing paper over, and draw over the outline on the reverse in pencil. Turn it back over and place it on top of the marine plywood. Trace over the front, transferring the design onto the board, ready to use the direct method as explained on page 10. There are four separate designs and two plain designs that do not need a template.

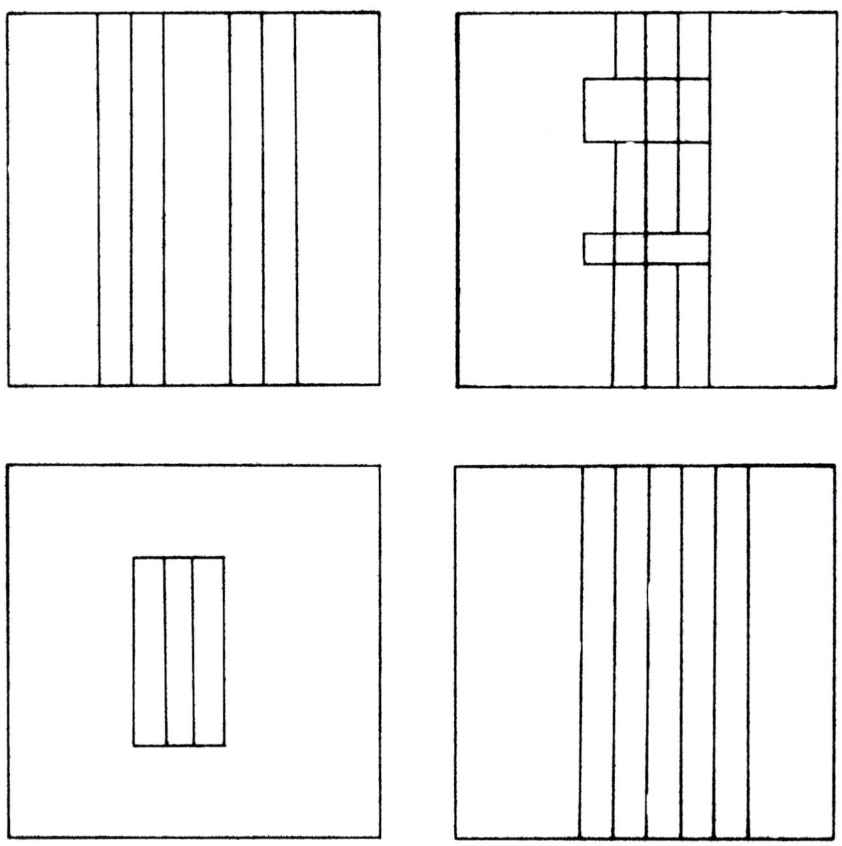

1 Remove the rough edges from all six pieces of plywood, using sandpaper and a block. Clean away the dust with a dry cloth. Apply a coat of PVA glue to the top and edges of the board and allow it to dry.

2 Leave the mosaics on the plastic or paper backing on which they are supplied and cut the sheet with scissors. Trace the template at the back of the book and place the tesserae into position on the tracing, one wall tile at a time.

3 Mix some adhesive and apply it onto the wood with a trowel; smooth down. Then drag the notched trowel back toward you at a 45° angle, making grooves. The grooves will provide a good tooth into which the tesserae can bond.

4 Transfer the marble line by line into the adhesive. Work on one tile at a time so that the adhesive doesn't dry out. You may need to use a ruler to keep the mosaic running in straight lines.

5 Once all six tiles are completed, allow them to dry for 24 hours. Clean with a damp sponge and remove excess adhesive with an awl or similar tool.

6 Apply a marble impregnator and protector with a clean paintbrush (read the manufacturer's instructions for drying time). Mix enough white powder grout for six tiles and apply using the grout float. Push the grout firmly into the spaces between the tesserae. Wipe away the excess grout with a damp sponge. Allow to dry for 24 hours.

7 Clean the tiles with a dry cloth to remove grout residue. Once the grout has dried, paint the edges and backs of the tiles a color of your choice (white was used for our tiles). Then varnish them for extra protection against all weather conditions.

8 Apply a marble color enhancer with a cloth and allow to dry. As the name suggests, this will bring out the color of the marble and protect it. If you have any queries, it is best to seek advice from your marble supplier.

INSPIRATIONAL IDEAS

These tiles could also be used as indoor wall hangings. You do not need to make all six. You could repeat the design and turn it into a beautiful floor pattern or kitchen backsplash—obviously, you would not need wood for this. They could also be made into tablemats and you could produce smaller versions for cups and glasses.

HINTS AND TIPS

- If you are experimenting with different mosaic colors or designs, make sure the type of mosaic you choose is suitable for exterior use and that the board is the correct size to fit all the tiles.
- Ask advice from a hardware store about the best method of attaching the tiles to the garden wall.
- Wash your paintbrush immediately after use to remove any PVA glue. Also wash adhesive and grouting tools after use.
- Apply PVA glue to the edges of the marine plywood because, although the wood is waterproof, any cut edges are not.
- Work on one tile at a time until you reach the grouting stage, which can be completed in one go.
- Before grouting, it is helpful to brush on a marble impregnator followed by a marble protector, available from most tile suppliers. These protect the marble from dirt and staining.
- Remove any adhesive that seeps over the side with a damp sponge.
- Read pages 7, 8, and 9 for advice on safety and mixing before starting this project.

Dolphin water feature

TOOLS AND MATERIALS

- Marine plywood: 4ft (1.2m) long x 2ft (60cm) wide x ½in (1cm) deep
- Tape measure and level
- Pencil and ruler
- Electric drill and countersink bit
- Screws: ½in (1cm)
- Sandpaper and block
- Tracing paper
- Waterproof PVA glue and paintbrush
- Unglazed porcelain tiles:
- cinca 1 x 1in (2.5 x 2.5cm); aqua tesserae ¾ x ¾in (2 x 2cm)
- Mosaic nippers
- Surgical and rubber gloves
- Safety glasses and mask
- Adhesive and additive
- Two buckets for mixing
- Trowel
- Tweezers
- Sponge and awl or similar tool
- White powder grout and additive
- Soft cloth
- Porcelain sealant and brush
- Two wooden battens: 4ft (1.2m) long x 2in (5cm) wide x 2in (5cm) deep
- Marine varnish
- Plastic wall anchors
- Screwdriver
- Water pump, metal grate, and reservoir bucket

PORCELAIN TESSERAE COLORS

Terra-cotta, Black, White, Cream, Beige, Aqua

The Romans loved water and bathing, and nearly all Roman villas contained a fountain or water feature of some kind. In this modern fountain, water flows from between the two dolphins' heads, almost as though it is coming from their mouths. These playful creatures are a popular motif and can be found all over the Roman world—a similar wall mosaic was created in Carthage, North Africa, in the 4th century b.c. Rather than using the more traditional marble, this mosaic is made from porcelain tesserae, which come in a wide variety of colors and tones that are well-suited to the Roman palette. Porcelain is also frostproof, which makes it ideal for use in a garden or sunroom. For a water feature of this kind, a pump should be installed with a reservoir beneath ground level.

Using the template

Trace the template at the back of the book using tracing paper. Turn the tracing paper over and draw over the outline of the design on the reverse in pencil. Turn it back over and place it on top of some brown paper. Trace over the lines once again, transferring the design onto the brown paper. If you are using an existing table, as in the example pictured here, you may find that the template does not cover the full tabletop. If so, use the direct method on page 10 to add a border around the template design, which should be positioned in the center.

1 Use a level and pencil to draw a center line along the board, from top to bottom. With the aid of a tape measure, make three marks along the board 2¾in (7cm) from the top. Join the marks to make a border line. Repeat 2in (5cm) from the bottom.

2 Drill screw holes for attaching the mosaic to the wall later. For a board that is 4ft (1.2m) long x 2ft (60cm) wide, drill six holes—three along the top and bottom edges.

3 Now drill through the holes with a countersink bit. This will produce a halo or circle around the edge of the hole, which will prevent the screwhead from protruding. Remove any rough edges with sandpaper and a block.

4 Trace the template (see Using the Template) so that you have two dolphins facing each other. Drill a hole for the water to come through in the space between the dolphins' noses. Coat the edges of the board with PVA glue using a paintbrush.

5 Cut the tesserae with mosaic nippers. Use quarters on the body and background, and smaller pieces on the tail, nose, and eye. Mix up some adhesive and trowel it onto small sections at a time. Use tweezers to position smaller pieces.

6 Complete the dolphins' bodies before moving onto the background. Make a halo around the dolphins using quarters of white tesserae. Work across the board, filling in the background. Finally, fill in the border and allow to dry for 24 hours. The drilled holes must be kept free of adhesive and tesserae. When dry, use an awl or similar tool to prick the mosaic free of any excess adhesive. Mix some white grout, and using a float, spread grout over the mosaic. Clean, polish, and allow to dry for 24 hours. Apply a porcelain sealant.

7 Coat the battens with marine varnish to protect them. You will need a friend to help you with the rest of this step and the next. Hold the mosaic against the wall where you want it to hang. Make sure it is straight by using a level. Draw lines to mark the top, bottom and sides of the mosaic position. Hold the first batten against the wall. The top should align with the top of the mosaic and it should not overlap the sides. Drill holes through the batten into the wall. Take the batten away and insert plastic wall anchors into the holes, then position the batten and fix. Use screws that are long enough to go through the batten and into the wall. Repeat with the second batten.

8 To attach the mosaic in place, position it on the battens. Ask a friend to help you hold the mosaic while you screw it to the battens. Once the screws are in place, mix some adhesive and stick the remaining tesserae onto the adhesive. Allow 24 hours to dry, then grout, clean, and polish.

HINTS AND TIPS

To create a water feature, dig a hole in the ground to make a reservoir in which the water can be collected—use a large bucket with a metal grate over the top. Pumps are available from garden centers. Full installation instructions will be provided, but you should seek advice from an electrician.

To change the size of the design, create a grid over the original design by drawing vertical and horizontal lines that are equally spaced. You can draw the next step directly onto the desired surface, but if you are likely to want to use the new design again, it is best to draw it onto paper or tracing paper first and then use that as a template. Draw an enlarged or decreased grid onto your surface or piece of paper. The grid must contain exactly the same number of squares, but the lines should be closer together or farther apart, depending on whether you are reducing or enlarging the image. Look at each individual square of the original design and transfer exactly what you see into the corresponding square on the new design. Alternately, you could resize the design on a photocopier.

INSPIRATIONAL IDEAS

One or both of these dolphins would make an ideal backsplash for a bathroom or could be used to decorate a shower or garden pond. Experiment with different color schemes and materials—blue and gold vitreous glass would work especially well with water.

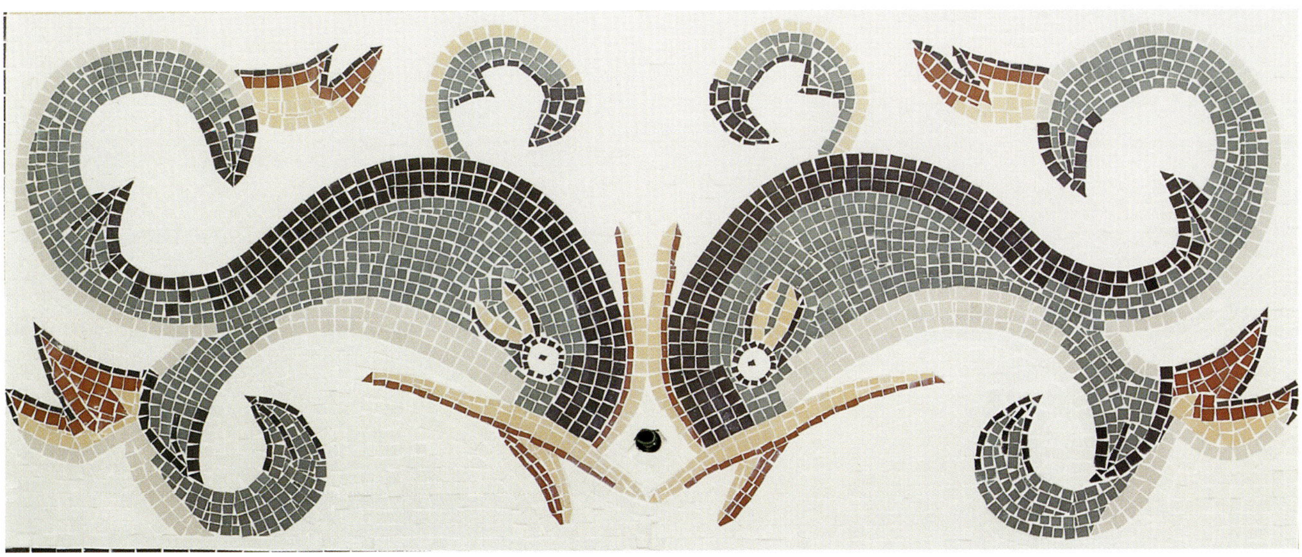

Roman knot paver

TOOLS AND MATERIALS

- Tracing paper
- Pencil
- Gummed brown paper, or plain brown paper and gum glue
- Cinca porcelain tesserae: 1 x 1in (2.5 x 2.5cm)
- Metal ruler
- Mosaic nippers
- Paintbrush
- PVA waterproof exterior glue
- Margin trowel
- Surgical and rubber gloves
- Safety glasses and mask
- Pavers with flat, smooth faces: 1⅓ x 1⅓ft (40 x 40cm)
- Notched trowel: ¼in (3mm)
- Adhesive and additive
- Two buckets for mixing
- Sponge
- Awl or similar tool
- White and gray powder grout and additive
- Grout float
- Cloth
- Porcelain sealant

PORCELAIN TESSERAE COLORS

- White
- Terra-cotta
- Black

Decorate your garden with these eye-catching mosaic pavers. Whether you arrange them in a group to create a focal point, or spread them out to make a path of stepping stones, they will bring color and interest to the garden through all the seasons. This ancient design, known as "Solomon's Knot," was extremely popular in Roman times, and often featured in floor mosaics. The twists and turns of the stylish knot pattern will serve as an elegant feature in any garden. This mosaic employs a typically Roman palette of terra-cotta, black, and white. Porcelain mosaics have been chosen because they are frostproof and ideal for exterior use. The indirect mosaic-laying method (see page 11) is ideal for this project.

Using the template

Trace the template at the back of the book. Turn your tracing paper over and draw over the outline of the design on the reverse in pencil. Turn it back over and place it on top of some brown paper. Trace over the lines once again, transferring the design onto the brown paper. Then follow the indirect method (see page 11) for laying the tesserae.

1 Trace the knot template at the back of the book and transfer it onto some brown paper. Make sure the paper has been cut to the size of the paver—in this example, 11/3 x 11/3ft (40 x 40cm).

2 Using a damp sponge on gummed brown paper or gum glue on plain brown paper, stick the black tesserae smooth side down around the edge to create a border. Line up the tesserae against a metal ruler to make sure they are straight.

3 Cut the terra-cotta and white mosaics into quarters using mosaic nippers (see page 8). Stick them onto the brown paper, starting from the center of the knot and working outward. Once the knot detail is complete, start on the edges using the white tesserae. Some of these will need to be cut into specific shapes to fit around the twists and turns of the design. To do this, hold the tesserae over the space, draw where the cut needs to be, and then cut. Allow the mosaic to dry for 24 hours.

4 Apply PVA glue with a paintbrush to the smooth upper side of the paver. Wear surgical gloves and wash the brush immediately after use.

5 Mix the adhesive and additive, and wearing surgical gloves, apply with a trowel. A margin trowel, which has a square head, is ideal for covering square areas. It is best to put the adhesive into the center, then spread and work it outward.

6 Once the paver has been covered with adhesive, use the trowel to smooth it down. Holding the notched trowel at a 45° angle, drag it toward you across the surface of the adhesive. Repeat this action over the entire paver.

7 Still wearing gloves, line the mosaic up with the edge of the paver and then slowly lower it face down onto the adhesive. You may find it easier if you get somebody to help with this stage of the process. Next, use your hands to smooth the tesserae firmly into place on the adhesive. This may cause excess adhesive to squeeze out around the edge but this problem is easily remedied—sponge off as much as you can while it is still wet, but do not worry if you cannot remove it all at this stage. Allow the mosaic to dry for 24 hours.

8 Gently wipe a damp sponge over the brown paper, which should start to come away from the surface. Peel back the paper to reveal the knot mosaic design underneath. Wash away any residue that is left behind.

9 Use an awl or similar tool to prick out any unwanted adhesive that may be attached to the tesserae. If it is showing through the gaps, it will still show even after the tiles have been grouted. Clean with a damp sponge.

10 Mix the grout in the ratio of 3 parts white to 1 part gray. Wearing rubber gloves, put some grout in the center and use a float to spread it into the corners. Once the paver is covered, remove any excess grout with the float.

11 Clean the mosaic with a damp sponge, then dry and polish with a cloth. Allow to dry for 24 hours. Once all the grime and dirt is removed, use a porcelain protector to seal the mosaic. Allow to dry and install in your garden.

INSPIRATIONAL IDEAS

This versatile design could be used on a wall or a piece of furniture, such as a table.

Published in 2005 by Bay Books, an imprint of Murdoch Books Pty Limited
Pier 8/9 23 Hickson Road, Sydney, NSW 2000
Phone: +61 (0) 2 8220 2000
Fax: +61 (0) 2 8220 2558

Murdoch Books UK Ltd
Erico House, 6th Floor North
93/99 Upper Richmond Road
Putney, London, SW15 2TG
Phone: +44 (0) 20 8785 5995
Fax: +44 (0) 20 8785 5985

www.murdochbooks.com.au

National Library of Australia Cataloguing-in-Publication Data
is available for this title.

ISBN-13: 978 1 74045 796 5
ISBN-10: 1 74045 796 X

Printed by Sing Cheong Printing Company Ltd. PRINTED IN CHINA.
First printed in 2005. Reprinted 2006 (twice).